MADE IN THE U.S.A.

CRAYONS

From Start to Finish

SAMUEL G. WOODS

PHOTOGRAPHS BY
GALE ZUCKER

BLACKBIRCH PRESS, INC.
WOODBRIDGE, CONNECTICUT

Special Thanks
The publisher would like to thank Eric Zebley,
Nancy McFarland, Nancy DeBellis, and Richard Sysko
for their generous help in putting this project together.

**If you would like to see crayons made, come to
The Crayola Factory® in downtown Easton, Pennsylvania.
For information call (610) 515-8000.**

Published by Blackbirch Press, Inc.
260 Amity Road
Woodbridge, CT 06525

e-mail: staff@blackbirch.com
Web site: www.blackbirch.com

Printed in Singapore

10 9 8 7 6 5 4 3 2 1

Photo Credits: All photos © Gale Zucker, except pages 7, 13
(lower right), 16, 17, 27 (top), 30, 31: courtesy Binney & Smith.
Artwork page 3: © Stephanie Singer and John Michael Brewer.
Courtesy Crayola Dream-Makers art collection.

Library of Congress Cataloging-in-Publication Data
Woods, Samuel G.
Crayons from start to finish / Samuel G. Woods : photographs by Gale
Zucker.—1st ed.
    p.   cm. — (Made in the U.S.A.)
    Includes bibliographical references.
    Summary: Text and photographs illustrate how crayons are made at the
Binney & Smith company in Easton, Pennsylvania, where an average of twelve
million crayons are produced every day.
    ISBN 1-56711-390-7
    1. Crayons—Juvenile literature. [1. Crayons.] I. Zucker, Gale.
II. Title. III. Series.
TS1268.W66   1999
741.2'3—dc21
                                               99-19434
                                                CIP
                                                  AC

CONTENTS

*"Woman Dancing"
by Richard Willis,
age 6: Ridge Hill
School, Hamden,
Connecticut.*

Above: "Animal Greetings" by John Michael Brewer, age 10: Seton Elementary School, North Sydney, Nova Scotia.
Right: "Super Clown" by Stephanie Singer, age 8: Maple West Elementary School, Williamsville, New York.

If you're like most kids, you have probably created something with crayons. You can find crayons in school, in your room, at your friend's house, even at some of your local family-style restaurants. Crayons are everywhere.

But what exactly is a crayon? And how does it actually get made?

Billions of Crayons

Binney & Smith, located in Easton, Pennsylvania, makes an average of 12 million Crayola® crayons every day. That means they make about 3 billion crayons a year. That's enough crayons to circle the earth 6 times!

It only takes a total of 3-5 minutes to make a crayon. In fact, that's all the time needed to make an average batch of 2,500 crayons.

A giant box of crayons sits on top of The Crayola Factory® building at Two Rivers Landing in downtown Easton, Pennsylvania. The Crayola Factory is a hands-on family discovery center that simulates crayon making. The main crayon-making plant is about 6 miles away.

Wax and Pigment

Crayons are made from two basic ingredients. The main ingredient is a kind of wax called *paraffin*. It's a lot like the wax that makes up a birthday candle. The second ingredient is called *pigment*. That's the material that gives a crayon its color. Crayola® crayons come in more than 100 different colors.

Powdered pigments (colors) are added to large amounts of liquid paraffin (wax) to make crayons.

*Freight cars filled
with hot liquid paraffin.*

Silos store the paraffin until it is ready for use.

A Train Full of Wax

Heated, liquid paraffin arrives at the crayon-making plant in freight cars. From the freight cars, the wax is pumped into large *silos* (containers) that store it and keep it hot until it is ready to use. From the silos, the paraffin is pumped into the plant as it is needed.

After pigment and paraffin are mixed, the liquid is poured onto a molding table.

Liquid Crayons

At The Crayola Factory®, at Two Rivers Landing in downtown Easton, a simulation of how crayons are made is done with a flatbed molding machine—like at the plant. Heated machines mix the liquid paraffin with pigment. The result is a hot, waxy liquid that can be poured easily.

Workers pour the hot crayon mixture onto the top of the crayon-molding tables. As they pour, the liquid fills the hundreds of holes that will mold the crayons. Cold water travels through tubes inside the mold. The water cools the wax down quickly.

As the hot paraffin mixture is poured by the flatbed mold operator, it fills hundreds of holes.

Workers smooth the surface of the molding machine to make sure each hole is filled.

11

Cool Crayons

After several minutes, the hot wax cools and turns solid. At that point, a large scraper on the flatbed molding machine is turned on. The scraper slides down the waxy lane and scrapes up all the excess wax. When it reaches the end of the table, there is a large pile of wax pieces. Extra wax is then scraped from the top of the machine.

A large scraper clears the lane of hardened wax.

On the automated rotary mold—at the crayon-making plant—wax is scraped as the crayon mold moves in a circular motion.

On the flatbed molding machine the excess wax is collected at the end of the table.

Unwanted Chunks

The excess wax pieces are collected and poured back into the hot wax kettle. In the kettle, the pieces become liquid once again. This liquid will be poured out and used for another batch of crayons.

When the crayons have cooled, they are raised from below. Once raised, they sit inside a removable crayon rack that can be carried to another work station. Each case holds 1,200 crayons.

Excess wax pieces are dumped back into the hot liquid wax kettle.

Once the crayons are cool, they are pushed up through the holes in the machine.

Doodles

- In the last 95 years, more than 100 billion Crayola® crayons have been made.

- Darlene Martin, a grandmother from Port Orchid, Washington, won the actual 100 billionth crayon and sold it back to Binney & Smith for a $100,000 bond. The crayon now resides in the Crayola Hall of Fame in Easton.

15

Edwin Binney

C. Harold Smith

1885 *Edwin Binney and cousin C. Harold Smith form a partnership called Binney & Smith. Their company produces red oxide pigment that is used as a barn paint and a black pigment (carbon) that is used to strengthen car tires.*

1900 *A newly opened Binney & Smith mill in Easton, Pennsylvania begins production of slate school pencils. Two years later, the company manufactures the first dustless school chalk, which becomes a great success.*

1903 The company makes the first box of eight Crayola® crayons, which is sold for a nickel. The box contains black, brown, blue, red, violet, orange, yellow, and green.

The name Crayola *is coined by Edwin Binney's wife Alice. It comes from "craie," the French word for chalk and "ola" from "oleaginous," which means oily.*

1958 The first box of 64 Crayola crayons debuts and is a huge success. The built-in sharpener is an added favorite.

1996 The 100 billionth crayon rolls off the production line at the crayon-making plant in Easton, Pennsylvania.

1998 The U.S. Postal Service honors Crayola crayons with a commemorative stamp. The stamp features the original box of eight that was first sold in 1903.

The first Crayola® 8-pack was sold in 1903.

17

The rack filled with crayons is lifted from the flatbed molding machine.

Tossing Crayons

At the second work station, the crayons are skillfully tossed from the rack. Experienced workers can get all 1,200 crayons to fly out onto the work table at once!

Now the crayons are ready to be sorted and inspected. Neat piles are created so workers can easily look over all the crayons at one time.

18

Tossing the crayons from the case for futher inspection.

Sorting

Stacking

Inspecting

Experienced workers can inspect hundreds of crayons at a time.

Ready for Inspection

Damaged or incomplete crayons are spotted by workers as they stack and sort the batches. Crayons that are not perfect are removed from the pile and thrown back into the kettle. There, they are re-melted and used to create a new batch.

Crayons that don't meet strict quality control standards are re-melted and re-used in a new batch.

21

Carrying and stacking before labeling.

Crayon Labels

With special paddles, the perfect crayons are moved to stock boxes. In the stock boxes, they await transportation to the labeling machine.

Crayons are placed on the labeling machine in large, single-color batches. On the machines, they roll down a ramp single file. Then, one by one, they fall into slots on a rotating wheel.

Large, single-color batches are loaded into the labeling machine. One by one, each rolls into a slot on a rotating wheel.

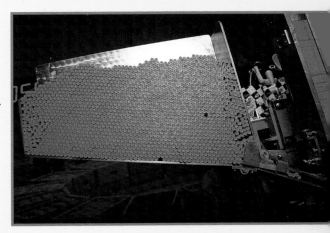

As the Wheel Turns

As the big labeling wheel turns, each crayon gets a double-wrapped label with the Crayola® logo and color name. Once a crayon is labeled, it rolls down onto a runway and into a collection bin.

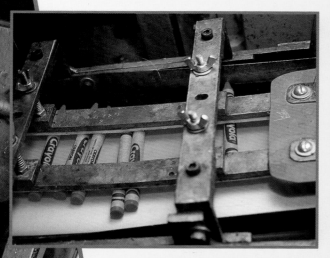

Finished crayons roll down a chute and onto a moving platform before they enter a large bin.

25

Rolling Along

As production continues, the crayons are sorted and stored by color. When they are ready to be boxed, they will be placed in large plastic dispensers. From those dispensers, each crayon will roll out onto a conveyor belt.

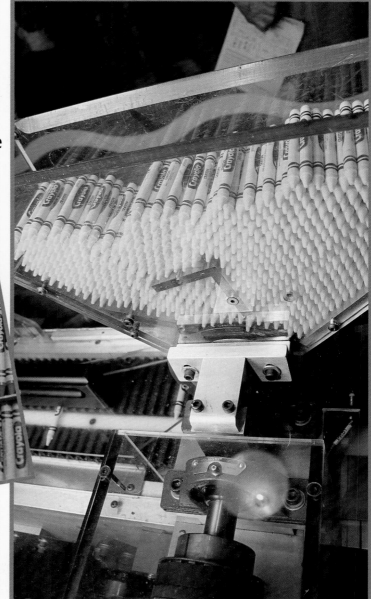

One at a time, each color joins the group, which travels down the line toward a box.

Heading toward the boxes.

From Belt to Box

When all the colors of a box of Crayola® crayons are on the belt, they are gently pushed into their package. They enter the box from the bottom. Then, as the box slides forward, it is folded closed.

Colors for a Crayola® crayon 4-pack are pushed into their box.

Filled boxes roll down the line for the final fold at the top.

Crayola® crayons are the world's most popular crayons.

Around the World

Finished boxes are loaded into cartons and are shipped all over the world. Crayola® crayons are sold in more than 80 countries, from Iceland to Belize. They are also packaged in 12 languages: English, French, Dutch, German, Italian, Spanish, Portuguese, Danish, Finnish, Japanese, Swedish, and Norwegian.

COLORFUL CRAYOLA® FACTS

🌀 If you put all the crayons that Crayola® produces in a year together, you'd have one giant crayon 37 feet (11 meters) wide and 120 feet (36.6 meters) taller than the Statue of Liberty!

🌀 The average child will wear down 730 crayons by his or her 10th birthday.

🌀 Kids ages 2-8 spend an average of 28 minutes each day coloring. Combined, kids in the U.S. spend 6.3 billion hours coloring each year. That's almost 10,000 human lifetimes!

🌀 In 1993, Crayola allowed people from the general public to name 16 new colors. More than 2 million suggestions were received. Some of the winners were: purple mountain's majesty, timber wolf, asparagus, tickle me pink, and tumbleweed.

🌀 Although Crayola crayons come in more than 100 different colors, the labels are only made in 18 colors.

🌀 Fred Rogers, of Mr. Rogers' Neighborhood, helped to make the 100 billionth Crayola crayon in July 1996.

Glossary

automated done by machines, not by people.

carbon a chemical element found in coal and in plants and animals.

conveyor belt a moving belt that carries objects from one place to another.

kettle a large metal pot used for boiling liquids.

paraffin a white, waxy substance that is used to produce crayons and candles.

pigment a substance that gives color to something.

rotating turning around and around in a circle.

silo a tall, round tower used for storage.

For More Information

BOOKS

Forman, Michael H. *From Wax To Crayon: A Photo Essay* (Changes). Danbury, CT: Children's Press, 1997.

Gibbons, Gail. *The Art Box.* New York, NY: Holiday House, 1998.

Jones, George. *My First Book of How Things Are Made: Crayons, Jeans, Guitars, Peanut Butter, and More* (Cartwheel Learning Bookshelf). New York, NY: Cartwheel Books, 1995.

Kain, Kathleen. Robert Byrd (Illustrator). *All About How Things Are Made* (Inspector McQ). Chicago, IL: World Book, Inc., 1995.

WEB SITE

Crayola Crayons Discover a coloring book, art, game room, story time, and fun crayon facts—www.crayola.com

Index